Sold.

The Questions & Answers for Selling Your Home Smoothly

By BETH BAKER OWENS

B B O PRESS

BBO PRESS
www.BethBakerOwens.com
Beth@BethBakerOwens.com

Books may be purchased in quantity and/or special sales by contacting the publisher directly.

BBO Press, 6130 S Kirk St, Centennial, CO 80016
Beth@BethBakerOwens.com

Editing by: Serena Billmayer, Lon Welsh, Joe Massey, Megan Beach, Kent Owens, Kelsey Owens
Cover Design & Interior by: Kelsey Owens: KAOS Studio

ISBN: 979-8-89379-173-0 (Soft Cover)
ISBN: 979-8-89379-172-3 (eBook)
LCCN: 2024910590

Non-Fiction | Real Estate | DIY | Business

First Edition

WELCOME!

Welcome homeowners, investors, personal representatives, and Realtors. You're interested in selling a home. A home is often a person's largest asset. The home may be where you raised your family or an investment or an estate. There are many reasons for selling a home. In the U.S., homeowners move about every 13 years. In the Denver Metro area, where I have worked since 1997, the average is 9 years between moves.[1]

This book is my distillation from selling hundreds of homes in all kinds of markets for you to use for your home sale. Each chapter has information and a worksheet to apply the lessons for your particular situation. Myths abound about how real estate works. That's where this book starts, Selling Myths. Next, the book explores the dynamic, inverse relationship between condition and price. Generally, a better condition brings a higher price. Buyers weigh if the

1 https://www.nar.realtor/blogs/economists-outlook/how-long-do-homeowners-stay-in-their-homes, Nadia Evangelou, Jan 2020 ,8)

changes that they think the property needs fit what they can do at the price a Seller asks for the property. This book separates condition and effective pricing, since they have different steps for the Seller. The next important detail is exposure–how effectively the home is marketed to the Buyers who value what the home offers. For a standard home in a standard neighborhood, the target is well defined. However, not every home sells with a standard approach. The last chapter covers how to regroup and sell a home that didn't sell the first time it was on the market. These homes are called withdrawn or expired listings because of how they are recorded in MLS. The MLS is the Multiple Listing Service, a centralized resource established and governed by Realtors to create a shared compilation of Realtors' listings for buyers and sellers.

If your home didn't sell the first time, perhaps you'll be able to learn some ways your next time around, that will result in a smooth move. When you prepare to sell your home, this book can be an invaluable resource as you consider how you can avoid pitfalls from common myths and work with reality by addressing condition, price and exposure for a sure selling process. This book does not address details of preparing nor negotiating a contract. Navigating a purchase contract through to closing is part of the art and science of a Realtor. What happens if a purchase contract fails is not addressed here either. Consult your Realtor and perhaps a real estate attorney for details about contracts and procedures. A purchase contract requires professional preparation and evaluation. With the right professionals on your team, you can navigate the contract details as smoothly as possible to a satisfactory closing.

Woven into these chapters are ways to prepare your home and target your Buyers to sell your home. First, we'll address common myths about selling. Then, we'll consider your home's condition. Next, we'll combine knowledge about your home, the market and price in your planning to set you up for success. In the following chapter, we'll address effective exposure of your home through thoughtful marketing, showings, and disclosures. Finally, if your home doesn't sell the first time, we'll discuss how you can regroup and get your property sold. After decades of working with Sellers in all kinds of markets, I know you can sell your home. Hopefully, ideas in this book will make the process smooth and straightforward for you, your Realtor and the others you engage to help with tasks throughout the process.

CONTENTS

MYTHS ABOUT SELLING & BUYING HOMES

Don't fall victim to these common myths about real estate transactions.

01 **Myth : This home will sell itself.** Fact: *The home is the start. Details of the purchase contract and the individuals involved make the transaction smooth, or not.*

02 **Myth: Homes at any price sell. Price is no object in this neighborhood.** Fact: *If money is exchanged, price matters.*

03 **Myth: You can price high and adjust down until you hit the right price.** Fact: *This bargaining process works, if the Seller is ok with Buyers wondering what's wrong with the home and why no one wanted it in the first place.*

04 **Myth: Just being in this neighborhood is enough.** Fact: *Location, condition, and price all matter to a Buyer.*

05 **Myth: Buyers always change the new flooring and paint.** Fact: *Few Buyers can imagine a home beyond what they see and smell. Even an artist prepares the canvas before painting.*

06 **Myth: Since I don't mind the issue... noise, power lines, traffic, trains, schools, neighbors, airports, pet smells, cracks, etc.; a Buyer won't either.** Fact: *To appeal to a broader variety of Buyers, address concerns others have raised about your home. Buyers usually care about the issue.*

07 **Myth: An investor will pay me lots of money for the home**. Fact: *Investors make their money by buying low and selling for a profit.*

08 **Myth: Online property value estimates and tax valuations tell the sales price of the property.** Fact: *Online property value estimates are only as accurate as the assumptions that are used in the mathematical models. Tax valuations are based on prices from the past and are made using properties from back then, with projected adjustments made for market changes.*

09 **Myth: There is no cost for buying first and selling next.** Fact: *This convenience comes at a cost in fees. Carrying costs and sometimes limited choices of lenders and title services are common.*

10 **Myth: All service providers: closing companies, appraisers, realtors, stagers, etc., are the same.** Fact: *They're not. Ask your Realtor which service providers they trust and why.*

11 **Myth: This home doesn't need an inspection.** Fact: *Protect yourself as a Seller, and encourage the Buyer to investigate the home.*

12 **Myth: A vacant home doesn't need any more maintenance.** Fact: *Problems in vacant homes usually go undetected for longer. For example, when a pipe breaks in a vacant home, the problem is often discovered after extra damage has occured.*

13 **Myth: As long as the home looks good, the photo quality is not important.** Fact: *Online photos and videos are a Seller's first showing.*

14 **Myth: Upgrades, remodeling, and lot premiums pay for themselves at resale.** Fact; *Especially for new builds the lot premiums are highest for the first Buyer. Later, there may be a higher value for being on the park or with an awesome view, but it will be a fraction of what was charged initially. If an upgrade makes the home more functional for you and brings you joy, then the cost could be worth it to you. The cost may not be worth it to the next Buyer.*

15 **Myth: Staging is an unimportant expense.** Fact: *Staging improves the emotional impact of the home for Buyers.*

16 **Myth: Buyers can see past the dirt, clutter, tenants, and pets.** Fact: *No. Buyers are easily distracted by these flaws and struggle to see your home for what it offers.*

17 **Myth: Homes don't sell in the winter.** Fact: *Ask your Realtor what the buying patterns are in your neighborhood.*

18 **Myth: Saving money on electricity, and heating or cooling is always important.** Fact: *Buyers want a comfortable home. If you aren't sure what is comfortable to others, look at model homes for lighting and comfortable temperature ideas.*

19 **Myth: Selling your home yourself is easy.** Fact: *Less than 8% of For Sale By Owners (FSBOs) sell their home without an agent and usually to a friend or a family member.*

20 **Myth: Selling a home means, you have to show it whenever anyone wants.** Fact: *There is a balance between accommodating showings and still living in your home. Ask your Realtor what is standard in your neighborhood.*

21 **Myth: My neighbors will bring me a buyer without an agent.** Fact: *This happens in rare cases for unique homes in highly desireable neighborhoods. This is not normal.*

22 **Myth: The highest price offer is the best.** Fact: *For Sellers, price is one of the considerations, balanced with timing, inclusions, exclusions, and contract terms.*

23 **Myth: Title insurance and an O&E are fluff costs.** Fact: *In some states, title insurance is required by law. An O&E (owner and encumbrance) report is a report that gives a Seller and Realtor a preliminary list of who holds title and what liens are filed against the property.*

24 **Myth: The Buyer's loan type doesn't matter.** Fact: *Some loans have additional requirements, identified by the appraisers, about the condition of the property. These can cause the Seller to perform specific work before the loan will be provided for the sale.*

25 **Myth: If this sounds too good to be true, it is your lucky day.** Fact: *Caveat emptor, buyer beware. This is why inspections, title reviews, appraisals, etc. are part of the purchase contract with possible. outs for the Buyer.*

26 **Myth: Once there is a signed contract, my home is sold.** Fact: *To quote Yogi Berra. " The game isn't over til it's over." There are many moving parts to getting a contract through closing.*

27 **Myth: Purchase contract contingencies only benefit the Buyer and give the Buyer an easy exit.** Fact: *Both Buyer and Seller have to perform specific tasks in a contract. Ask your Realtor or lawyer how the contingencies affect you.*

28 **Myth: The Seller doesn't have to disclose old inspection details.** Fact: *The Seller is required to disclose known defects to avoid misunderstandings and accusations, by the Buyer, of fraud. Disclose, disclose, disclose.*

29 **Myth: The inspection report is a repair list for what has to be fixed.** Fact: *An inspection report includes commentary about current codes, how systems functioned during the inspection, and general information about best practices. Some items will not be deemed important enough to be addressed by either Buyer and Seller.*

30 **Myth: If the purchase contract closes after the first of the month, the seller doesn't need to pay that month's utilities bills, HOA dues, or mortgage.** Fact: *Bills are still due on time. Any overage received by the utility, mortgage company, or HOA will be returned after closing to the Seller.*

31 **Myth: If I have a Realtor, I don't ever use an attorney.** Fact: *While Colorado doesn't require the use of an attorney, some states require them for specific parts of a real estate transaction. Certain deeds, like a personal representative deed for an estate, are prepared by an attorney. Ask your Realtor.*

32 **Myth: The Buyer can move in before closing.** Fact: *This is seldom advisable, in case the sale doesn't close on time or something happens to the home before closing.*

33 **Myth: The Seller has to be moved out at time of closing.** Fact: *It is common practice in some places for the Seller to be moved out when they sign their closing documents, but not in Colorado. A rent back can also be used to allow the Seller to stay in the property after closing, as a renter for up to 59 days.*

34 **Myth: There is only one way to negotiate a purchase contract.** Fact: *There are standard practices. As long as the written agreement is legal and both sides agree, variations can be made. Lenders and title closers have strict standards for closing.*

35 **Myth: In a Seller's Market, Buyers don't get to choose the price they want to pay.** Fact: *Buyers choose if they want to purchase a property, or not, at the going price. In a bidding war, a Buyer can remove the offer from the table.*

36 **Myth: There is only one way to negotiate through a purchase contract.** Fact: *As long as it is legal, everything is negotiable in some cases. However, there is a standard contract that a Realtor is supposed to use as a template. Only an attorney may write contracts from scratch.*

37 **Myth: In a Seller's Market, Buyers don't get to choose the price they want to pay.** Fact: *The Buyers can and do choose the price they will pay.*

38 **Myth: In a Buyer's Market, any offer works for a Seller.** Fact: *Some offers do not meet the Sellers bottom line of price and terms.*

39 **Myth: You have to accept the first offer that is made.** Fact: *Except in small markets, there is more than one Buyer for a home over time.*

40 **Myth: Open houses sell houses. In low inventory situations, an open house may attract a frustrated Buyer.** Fact: *Usually neighbors and people just starting their process attend open houses.*

41 **Myth: Walk scores are ableist and against fair housing.** Fact: *Walk scores give a sense of how close schools, parks, restaurants, entertainment, mass transit, etc. are to the property. It's a lifestyle measurement.*

42 **Myth: There are no additional costs when selling a residence.**
Fact: *There may be capital gains or sales tax or special assessments that are due a closing. Ask your Realtor, CPA, HOA or Metro District about these.*

CH.1 PREPARE YOUR HOME

CONDITION AFFECTS PRICE & TIME TO SELL

When you have emotionally decided to move and sell your home, the labor begins. Most Sellers want to sell in the shortest amount of time, for the highest net. They want the most flexibility in moving, and the least angst. Moving is hard work. It's emotional to have your space invaded and evaluated by others, too. Your goal is to prepare your home and balance the amount of cost and work against the expected return in ease of selling and net profit.

As a child, my grandfather was a collector of mechanical items, minerals, jewelry, and more. He was always buying and selling items. He taught me some important lessons in selling, as he prepared for his collecting trips. He stressed the importance of having everything clean and in working condition before you show it to a potential Buyer. He would lovingly prepare his items for sale by depersonalizing them, stripping them down, cleaning them up, making sure they worked properly.Then he would add a little glamour by making them shiny and a little special. He did all this in anticipation of attracting Buyers who would also love the now sparkling treasure.

Grandpa's principles apply to selling homes, too. When preparing your home for sale, it's important to start with stripping down the clutter in your home and giving it a thorough cleaning. Then, make sure the home is well maintained. Finally, consider adding a little glamour and sparkle. There are now some tech tools to help with the process, but the hard work and principles remain the same.

MAKE IT SPARKLE.

STRIP DOWN TO THE HOUSE

You're selling a property, right? You want people focused on your property, not distracted by what is in it.

SORT & DECLUTTER

Begin by going through each room and sorting your belongings into categories: sell, donate, throw away, and keep. Be honest with yourself about what you truly need and what can be let go. Get rid of old furniture you don't want to move; home stagers suggest removing 1/3 of your furniture and 1/2 of your clothes. This helps create a sense of space and make your home more appealing to potential Buyers. Even when selling "as-is", an empty home sells for a higher price than a cluttered home.

DEPERSONALIZE

Pack away family photos, awards, sayings, symbols of your religion or ideology. You are neutralizing the property so another person can imagine moving into it and living there with their belongings. Remember, you are selling the building and lot, not your family, their achievements, and their points of view. A Seller wins when the Buyer is focused on what they will do in the home, not distracted by who lives there now.

REMOVE SPECIAL ITEMS

Pack away expensive art, sports memorabilia, decorations, jewelry, guns, collections, etc. Sometimes a home is cased for items when it is for sale. While burglaries are uncommon, it is prudent to remove these special items from the home for safety's sake. Remove the special items before photos are taken and during your selling period.

HOARDER

BEFORE

Years of clutters and mess accumilated to created caverns of stuff.

CLEANED OUT

DURING

After weeks of decluttering and deep cleaning, the house is still left with residual stains.

FLIPPED

AFTER

With new baseboards and flooring, followed by a fresh coat of paint, the house is finally ready for market.

CLEAN IT UP

CLEAN OUT STORAGE AREAS

Clear out any excess items from closets, cabinets, attics, garage, and storage spaces. Buyers are interested in seeing ample storage potential, so make sure these areas are tidy, organized and not full.

PACK NON-ESSENTIAL ITEMS

As you declutter, pack away items that you won't need while your home is on the market. This will help create a cleaner and more spacious feeling.

CONSIDER STORAGE OPTIONS

If you have a significant amount of items that you don't want to part with and won't be using during the selling process, there are answers. Consider renting a storage unit or pod or utilizing organized space in your basement or garage. This will keep your home clutter-free and visually appealing.

Clean.

This is the general cleaning you do before company comes with extra attention to the common areas, the entrance, and the shared bath.

Wall Cleaning.

The large surfaces have a greater impact on what people perceive in a room. Remove cobwebs and marks. Some areas may need washing. Kitchen walls may need a degreaser to clean accumulated cooking grease. Bathroom walls may need extra scrubbing to remove soap scum, hard water spots, and grime in hard to reach places.

Floor Cleaning.

Consider having the carpets professionally cleaned before showing the home. Scrub tile and linoleum floors to remove the dirt in the grout and in textures on the surface. Clean floors improve the overall appearance and freshness of the home, making it more appealing to buyers.

Deep Cleaning.

This includes stairway handrails, windows, sills, countertops, cabinets, appliances, bathroom fixtures, shelves. Wipe down ceilings, baseboards, window coverings, handles, switches, vents, lights, fans, under cabinets, around toilets and refrigerators, etc. Would a white glove show dirt or grime if it touched anywhere? In our home we call that level of white glove cleaning Grandma Clean. Consider hiring professional cleaners if needed, as they can ensure a meticulous and spotless result.

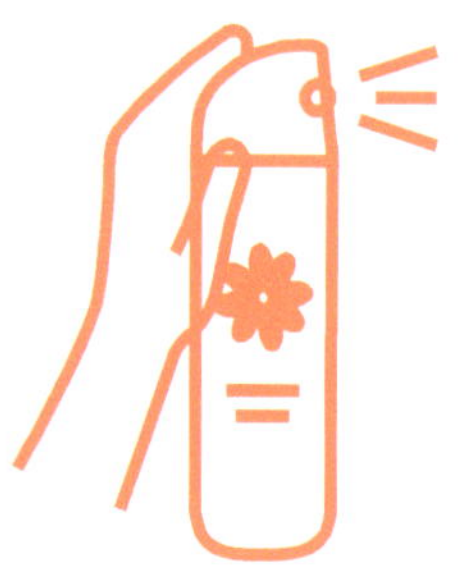

Deodorizing.

If there are lingering smells after cleaning, use baking soda or a glass of distilled vinegar to absorb odors. A stronger absorbent is charcoal or one of the products from NoOdor.com. For stronger smells, deodorize with ozone, following the safety precautions. Another way to deodorize is to remove the smelly object, say old flooring or curtains. Often after removing surfaces damaged by water, mold, pet urine, etc, the remaining underlying surfaces need to be treated with the appropriate sealant chemicals. For example, oil based KILZ will seal a subfloor after padding and carpet are removed. There are other industrial deodorizers applied by remediation companies for extreme problems.

By following these steps, you'll be well on your way to preparing your home for the market. Remember, a decluttered, organized, and clean home will attract more potential buyers and fetch a higher price.

How can you have your home pass the white glove test?

MAKE IT WORK PROPERLY

Maintenance matters to people buying a home. Disrepair deters most Buyers. They start wondering what repairs would cost. Start with a list of deferred maintenance in the home. Complete that honey-do list. Even when selling a home "as-is", little fixes can help a Buyer feel better about the home. Don't let your home suggest the Buyer could expect costly problems. When you hire someone to work on the home, save the receipts to provide to the Buyer later.

Depending on your budget, time and target Buyer, areas to maintain may include:

HVAC

HEATING, VENTILATION & A/C

Have the furnace and cooling systems cleaned, serviced, and maintained. If it is not working properly, replace it or repair it. If there is a gas leak, get that fixed right away for safety's sake.

PLUMBING

SEWER & WATERLINES

Have the sewer line cleaned and scoped. If line is cracked and leaking, turn off the water or have the line repaired or replaced. Contact your homeowner insurance about the issue.

ROOF

If you have had hail or the roof is older, have the roof inspected. Ask the roofer what would be needed for a 5 year roof certification, in case you need one during the inspection phase of a purchase contract later. Contact your homeowner insurance about wind or hail damage.

ELECTRICAL

If your home was built in the 1960's or 1970's, it may have aluminum wiring. Aluminum wiring sometimes gets hot at receptacles and fires can start. Consider having an electrician alter the connections to reduce chance of overheating at receptacles. If there are other electrical problems, have them fixed by an electrician. If there is no power when you start showing the property, notify your Realtor to alert showing agents.

WATER LEAKS

Repair any active leak and fix the water damaged area. If the heat is off in cold weather, turn off the water and have the plumbing winterized. Notify your Realtor if the water is turned off in the property, so the showing agent knows not to allow anyone to use the plumbing when touring the home. Contact your homeowner insurance about issues the homeowner insurance might cover, such as damage due to hail or flooding.

DETECTORS

Test your smoke detectors and carbon monoxide detectors. Ask your Realtor about where to place detectors if you are replacing them or if none are installed.

TILE

Caulk around water areas and regrout your tile where needed.

WOOD

Clean and brighten your wood floors, doors, trim and cabinets with a product like Murphy Oil Soap, Liquid Gold, or tung oil for woodwork. Use Rejuvenate, Murphy Oil Soap or Bona for floors.

ADJUST MOVING PARTS

Fix door latches and locks, floor squeaks, loose boards, sticky or drafty windows and doors, loose hinges, sticky doors, garage door springs.

WINDOWS

Repair or board broken windows. Fix torn or broken screens.

STEPS & DECK

Make the deck and steps safe. Or block them off, so no one is hurt during a showing.

HOLES

Patch holes in walls. Hollow core doors often cannot be repaired.

PESTS

Have them removed or exterminated.

Beyond basic maintenance there are updating and remodeling projects that can greatly enhance the appeal and value of your home. There is a limit to the return on each project. Over-improving a property means spending more money and time than is needed to get top dollar. Here are some considerations when deciding which projects to tackle.

PAY ATTENTION TO CURB APPEAL

This gives excellent return on your investment. You start to have a favorable impression of your home by presenting it attractively when Buyers first arrive. The exterior of your home is the first thing potential Buyers will see, so make sure it looks inviting and well-maintained. Trim bushes and trees, mow the lawn, rake the leaves and flower beds, plant flowers, and repair any visible damage. Enhancing the curb appeal will create a positive first impression.

ADD A LITTLE GLAMOUR

CREATE A WELCOMING ENTRANCE

The front door area is another crucial aspect of curb appeal. Buyers gather at the door for a while as their Realtor unlocks the door. Make sure the lock unlocks easily. A welcoming entryway is clean, without cobwebs and trash. The door is in good condition and works properly. Remove non-essential furnishings and decorations, so there is room for people to gather comfortably. Add some welcoming touches like a fresh doormat and shoe tray or booties.

FINISH UNFINISHED PROJECTS

If you have any ongoing projects or repairs, it's important to finish them before listing your home. Potential buyers may be deterred by seeing unfinished work. Completing these projects will present your home in its best light and help you get top dollar.

CONSIDER LOCAL RETURN ON INVESTMENT (ROI)

Different projects have varying return on investment depending on your local market and neighborhood. Research the average ROI for different remodeling projects in your area to determine which ones are worth the investment. For example, kitchen and bathroom renovations tend to have higher returns compared to other projects. Ask your Realtor for this information.

KNOW THE STANDARD IN YOUR NEIGHBORHOOD

Take a look at other homes in your neighborhood to get an idea of the standard of updates and finishes. While you don't want to exceed the neighborhood standard, it's important to meet it to attract buyers. For example, if most homes in your area have updated kitchens, it might be worth considering a kitchen remodel or planning to adjust the price down for that cost.

FOCUS ON HIGH-IMPACT AREAS

Focus on areas that have a significant impact on Buyers' first impressions. Kitchens, bathrooms, walls and flooring are often important areas to invest in. These updates can help create a fresh and modern look that appeals to potential Buyers. Sometimes lights and window coverings have a high impact, too.

CONSULT WITH A REALOR

Consider seeking advice from a Realtor who knows your local market. They can provide valuable insights on which updates are in demand and which will yield the best returns. They can also help you determine a budget for your remodeling projects and help with getting contractors.

Remember, it's important to strike a balance among cleaning, updating, and avoiding over-improvement.

Consider your budget, the potential return on investment, and the preferences of Buyers in your area to make informed decisions about which projects to do.

When looking at all these steps and potential projects, Sellers often wonder how long it will take to get their homes ready to sell. It depends on what shape it's in now and how you want to position it in the market. If you are selling the home of a deceased hoarder, cleanout may be what you choose to do. If you're moving after being in the home for decades and have not updated the place, it might take you up to a year to prepare for top dollar. If you just want to sell, a cleanout and clean up may only take a month or so. If you are a meticulous homeowner who recently got rid of everything that doesn't bring you joy and remodeled the key areas in the last few years, you could list your home after a slightly deeper cleaning than normal in about a week. Remember, good condition increases price, decreases time on the market, and makes the transaction smoother.

HOME PREPARATION CHECKLIST

- All Areas
- Main Area
- Dining Room
- Bathrooms
- Exterior
- Kitchen
- Bedrooms

Is Your Home Ready to Sell?

ALL AREAS

01 Declutter all areas.

02 Clean, clean, clean all areas and surfaces.

03 Repair damages and items that need maintenance.

04 Decide what projects are worth your time and money to address now.

05 Make the home a neutral canvas for the Buyer to start mentally moving in.

DEEP CLEAN

EXTERIOR

01 Remove cars from driveway.

02 Close and clean all windows.

03 Power wash the exterior.

04 Scrape, repair, and paint any areas with peeling paint; repair any stucco.

05 Sweep walkways.

06 Pick up leaves, sticks, branches, and animal poop.

07 Remove dead plants, trim trees, and weed garden area.

08 Add fresh mulch to flower beds and manicure lawn.

09 Freshen up your porch and front door with new paint and removing clutter.

10 Put away toys, bicycles, yard care equipment, etc.

11 Fix fences and gates.

12 Store any out-of-season décor appropriately.

13 Make the outdoor living area welcoming.

MAIN AREA

01 Have all areas of your home looking and smelling fresh, so it feels inviting and move-in ready.

02 Deep clean all surfaces from floor to ceiling and everything in between. This includes the furnace, water heater, and other appliances that buyers will be checking out.

03 Remove personal items, photos, personal awards, memorabilia. The home is the star of the tour.

04 Remove all visible clutter.

05 Remove as much as 1/3 of your furniture and decorations.

06 Pack what you don't need now, including clothes, extra supplies, toys, books, kitchen items, etc.

07 Place boxes out of the way, perhaps in storage.

08 Neutralize colors.

09 Touch up woodwork and paint.

10 Repair water damage, wall damage, and complete other deferred maintenance.

MAIN AREA

11 Organize all closets, basements, and other storage areas.

12 Eliminate pet smells, pet hair, and damage by pets.

13 Fix lighting problems with additional lamps and fresh bulbs.

14 Open curtains and turn on all lights for showings.

15 Keep home temperatures at a comfortable for showings.

16 Empty waste baskets, put away kid and pet items, and tidy up before showings.

17 Vacuum carpets and sweep hard floors before showings.

18 Remove mail, newspapers, stray papers, and anything with personal information.

19 Display a few carefully chosen, attractive books or decorations.

20 Turn off the television, unless you are streaming music.

21 Create a focal point in each room that appeals to your target buyers.

KITCHEN

01 Wipe down all appliances, counters, cabinets, and ceilings.

02 Remove magnets from refrigerator doors.

03 Clean out the refrigerator.

04 Store food in cabinets.

05 Declutter counters, stove, and tables.

06 Stow small appliances.

07 Hide soaps and cleaning supplies.

08 Hide dish towels and sponges.

09 Clear sink of dishes.

10 Put away drying rack.

11 Organize items on open shelves.

12 Place a bowl of fruit or something fresh on the counter or table.

DINING ROOM

01 Straighten dining room chairs.

02 Add a centerpiece with flowers or candles.

03 Set the table for dinner.

04 Add a bottle of wine or cider and glasses.

BEDROOMS

01 Make the beds.

02 Arrange decorative pillows.

03 Put away clothes and shoes.

04 Clean under the beds and dressers.

05 Clear surfaces of clutter.

06 Put away children's toys.

BATHROOMS

01 Clean the bathrooms and surfaces so they "sparkle".

02 Hang fresh towels.

03 Remove toiletries from the counter.

04 Clean mirrors.

05 Clean the toilet, around the toilet, and close the lid.

06 Remove all extraneous items from tubs and showers.

07 Open the shower curtains.

CH. 2 SET UP FOR SUCCESS

When preparing to sell your home, you have options that can position your home to be the one with better bids, more favorable terms and back up offers. You can set yourself up for success. Work with your Realtor as a team on these topics.

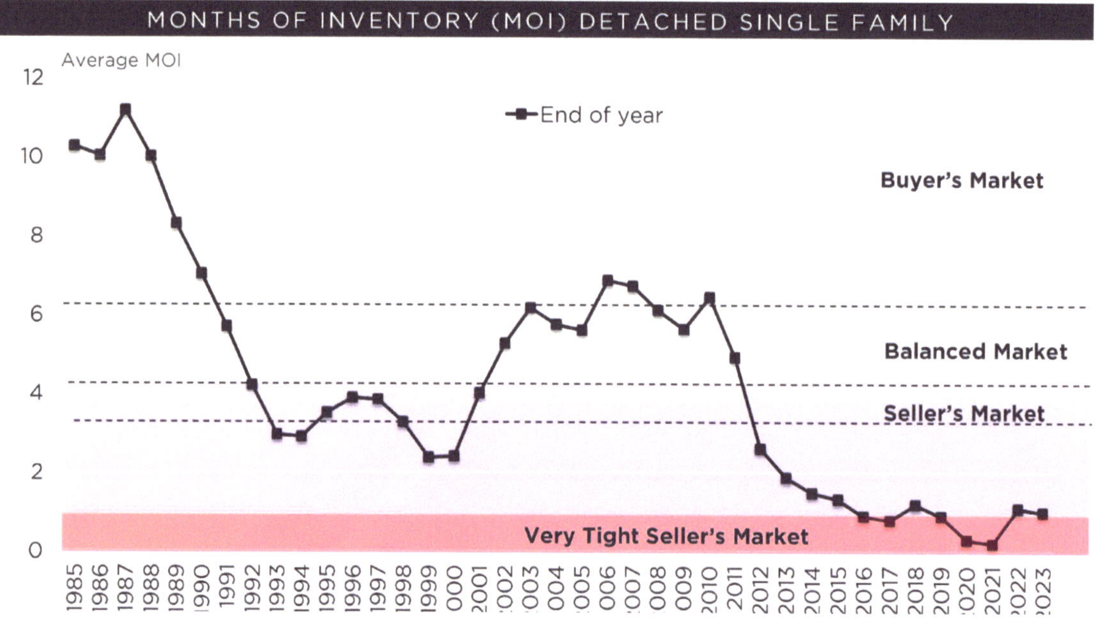

MARKET CONDITIONS

Have your Realtor share the current days on market in your neighborhood, the expected rate of showings and how many showings are usual before most homes get under contract. Tailor your marketing strategy to the prevailing market conditions. In a seller's market, aim for multiple offers and consider seeking backup offers when negotiating the purchase contract. In a buyer's market, focus on reducing negative triggers (such as odors or dark rooms) and adding positive emotional triggers (such as pleasant smells, seller concessions, and staging) to appeal to potential Buyers.

PRE-INSPECTION

Consider getting an inspection done before listing your home. This will help identify any potential issues that Buyers may discover during their own inspection. Addressing these issues beforehand can help streamline the selling process and prevent surprises. However, problems the inspector identifies need to be disclosed to potential Buyers. Ask your Realtor about the required disclosures.

HOME WARRANTY

Offering a home warranty can be an attractive incentive for Buyers and might cover you while you are listing your home for sale, too. A home warranty provides owners and Buyers reassurance that specific systems and appliances in the home will be covered by the policy in case of unexpected repairs or failures. Newly constructed homes offer warranties, so a home warranty helps a resale property compete better. Not all warranties are the same and the fine print matters when learning what is covered and for how much. Ask your Realtor about home warrenties.

PROFESSIONAL CLEANING

Consider advertising that your home will be professionally cleaned after you move out. This ensures that the home is in its best possible condition when they move in. Many Buyers are uncomfortable thinking about settling into another person's dirt.

CARPET CLEANING

Consider advertising that your carpets will be professionally cleaned after you move out to assure the Buyers they can move in right after closing.

EXCELLENT PHOTOS

Invest in professional photography to showcase your home. Good lighting and open window coverings helps the photographer showcase your home. HD photos and twilight filters add depth to your photos. HD is high definition, better quality, with fewer shadows and lack of definition. Consider including drone photos and neighborhood photos to highlight the property and the lifestyle the location offers.

CLEAR DESCRIPTION

Have your Realtor craft a clear and engaging description of your home, highlighting its unique features and the lifestyle it offers. Avoid mentioning protected classes to ensure compliance with fair housing laws. Choose pictures and descriptions that appeal to your target Buyers. Apply this understanding to how you stage specific areas of the house. Ask your Realtor or stager how to set those positive triggers in the home.

IDENTIFY SELLING POINTS

Reflect on what qualities initially attracted you to the home when you bought it. Have your Realtor include those aspects in the marketing efforts. Focus on the lifestyle that the location and home provide. Buyers choose homes based on lifestyle more than the features listed.

ADDRESS PROPERTY ISSUES

Identify the five most bothersome problems about the property and address them, either through repairs or disclosures. Being proactive can alleviate concerns for potential buyers.

FINANCIAL CONSIDERATIONS

Determine how much you owe on your mortgage, line of credit (HELOC loan), down payment assistance loan, HOA special assessments, and any other outstanding payments. Consider what else you want to pay off at closing. Calculate your desired profit and potential capital gains tax implications. Ask your CPA, Financial Planner, and Realtor if there are any additional taxes for your home sale. This will prepare you to better negotiate offers when they arrive.

TIMING CONSIDERATIONS

Discuss your first choice and alternative choices for timing for your move with your Realtor. Many neighborhoods have hotter selling seasons. Some neighborhoods have little seasonality in home sales.

COMPLETE PAPERWORK

Gather all receipts and property paperwork in one place, including the Seller's property disclosure (SPD) and lead based paint disclosure (LBP). Having organized documentation will facilitate the disclosure part of the selling process.

RELOCATION SERVICES

Discuss any corporate relocation benefits you have and the people to contact about your specific corporate relocation procedures. There are often additional paperwork and steps required for a relocation transaction. Sometimes, the corporation buys out the Seller and becomes the Seller. This changes some of the contract requirements, but usually not the preparation and marketing exposure.

BEFORE STAGING

VIRTUAL OR TRADITIONAL STAGING

Consider the benefits of virtual staging and traditional staging to enhance the visual appeal of your home. Staging can help Buyers envision themselves living in the space. When selling lifestyle, staging is crucial. Staging can make a significant difference in attracting offers. In 2023 Profile of Home Staging, the National Association of Realtors found 48% of staged homes sell much faster than unstaged homes and 34% of staged homes sold for 1-10% more money. Staging can focus Buyers' attention on possible lifestyles in the home and improve their emotional connection with the home. If you choose virtual staging, have your Realtor include an untouched photo, too, so people understand the virtual staging is a suggestion.

AFTER STAGING

UTILIZE TECHNOLOGY

Explore the possibility of using 3D tours or other virtual tour options to provide an immersive online experience for potential buyers. These tools can increase engagement and interest in your listing. There are tools for some video tours that allow a person to change colors of walls and flooring to design a look they might want in the home. Others allow a person to add models of their furniture to see how it would fit.

COMMUNICATION WITH YOUR AGENT

Discuss various scenarios and "what ifs" with your Realtor in advance. This includes potential changes in house prices, time deadlines, alternative plans, early move-outs, and market fluctuations. Being prepared will help you make informed decisions throughout the selling process.

SHOWING LOGISTICS

Determine how showings will be scheduled, who will handle them, and the time windows available. Address any considerations for people working from home, sleeping children, or day sleepers. Establish protocols for managing showings when people knock on the door unexpectedly. During a yard sale you may choose to hand out your Realtor's card, rather than have an open house. Sometimes virtual showings better serve the Seller and Buyer when providing accessibility.

SECURITY AND PETS

Develop a plan to ensure the security of valuable items, firearms, and controlled medicines during showings. Also, consider how to handle pets during showings, whether it's removing them from the premises or making arrangements to keep them in a designated area.

By considering these points, you can set yourself up for a successful home selling experience and address various aspects that can impact the sale of your home.

ADDITIONAL TRANSFER DETAILS

HOA special assesments, deed restrictions, mineral rights, water rights, encumbered inclusions, leased inclusions: all need to be addressed during a transaction. Work with your Realtor on these items, before listing. Some common examples include solar panels, security systems, and propane tanks.

UESTIONS FOR SUCCESS

- Affecting Price
- About Marketing
- Paperwork and Process
- Additional Incentives

By asking better questions, you can better prepare to place your home in the market where it will sell more easily and for more money. Go over these with your Realtor.

AFFECTING PRICE

01 What are current market conditions and how do they affect my home sale now? If I put my home on the market later, how is the market trending?

02 If my home is priced correctly, what can I expect for showings? For offers?

03 What are my possible returns for selling at different levels of condition (repair and updating)? Look at different projected net sheets to compare.

04 What would be an optimum offer (price, terms, timing, etc)? What is my next best alternative offer?

05 What if the home doesn't sell right away? How would you as my Realtor handle price and marketing changes?

PAPERWORK & PROCESS

01 Is there any paperwork we need to proceed (Letter of Testamentary, mortgage information, HOA information, corporate relocation documents, etc)? For closing (trust documents, Power of Attorney)?

02 Ask the Realtor: How often and how will we communicate about timing for photos? Showings? Feedback? Adjustments? Offers? Other things that may come up?

03 How many homes do you sell? What areas do you serve? What expertise do you have that would serve me in this transaction?

04 What else do I really want to know about selling and moving?

ADDITIONAL INCENTIVES

01 What does a pre-inspection cost? What are my risks and benefits for having this done?

02 What home warranties are affordable yet provide good coverage? Am I competing with new builds for the same Buyers?

03 How would handing over an immaculate home sway Buyers in my market?

ABOUT MARKETING

01 Who are the likely Buyers for my home? What are their lifestyles and their concerns? How can I address these by preparing, staging, and in marketing my home?

02 How do you market my property to expose it to likely Buyers while addressing known problems up front?

03 What additional photos, tours, and other tech assistance will get my home better exposure?

04 What are the problems with this property and how will my Realtor and I address them for the Buyers?

05 What are the benefits of this property and how will my Realtor and I address them for the Buyers?

06 How can we make showings as available as possible with my current living/ working parameters?

"Good fortune is what happens when opportunity meets with planning."

- THOMAS EDISON, INVENTOR

CH. 3 SNAG THE BUYER

Effective Exposure for Virtual & Live Showings

In today's world on-line listings are shared broadly across the web. Your first showing is virtual and could happen on a variety of platforms that each present the information in their own way. The MLS has the most complete information and is the best resource. Data transferred from MLS to other platforms is not always consistent. For this reason the description and photos are especially important. When a Realtor makes an appointment to see your home live, it is for a second or third showing! Here are some additional tips to consider when accommodating live showings and enhancing the overall presentation of your home.

PRIORITIZE LIVE SHOWINGS

Be flexible and accommodating with scheduling live showings to allow potential Buyers to easily see the property in person. A repeated live showing provides an opportunity for Buyers to spend even more time exploring the home and envisioning themselves living there. This is the time to roll out the red carpet of welcome.

PROMINENT SIGNAGE

Place a visible and well-maintained "For Sale" sign in front of your property to make it easily identifiable to interested Buyers and their agents. It helps the neighbors with word of mouth marketing, too.

INFORMATION AVAILABILITY

Provide easily accessible information about your home, such as a flyer with a QR code or a dedicated website, where potential Buyers can find detailed information, photos, and virtual tours. Understand that there are many online resources, including AVM (automatic valuation models). No AVM says what your listing price should be. Buyers will look at the AVM and want to know why your price is different.

MAINTAIN CLEANLINESS

Keep your home extra clean throughout the selling process. Daily tidy up, dust, vacuum, put away dishes and take out the trash. Before showings ensure that all areas are presentable for potential Buyers.

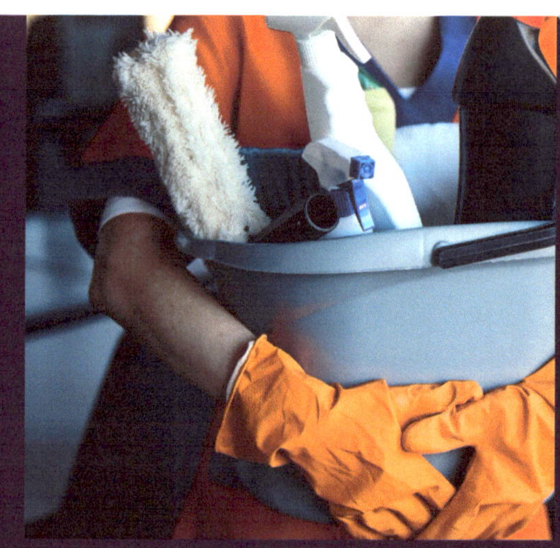

CONSIDER FIRST OFFERS

While the first offer may not always be perfect, it's worth considering. Evaluate the terms and conditions carefully. Consult with your Realtor to make an informed decision as you negotiate. While everything is negotiable, not every Buyer is flexible in all areas, and nor are you.

UPDATE DISCLOSURES

The rule of thumb is "disclose, disclose, disclose". Does the property have any deed restrictions? These must be disclosed to potential Buyers. When there are any changes or new information, update your Seller's disclosures accordingly. Additionally, after inspections, make sure to update the disclosures based on the findings from the inspection. If you have different information than what the inspector found, include that in your disclosures, too. Sometimes reports and reciepts are also helpful to provide to Buyers. Consult your Realtor for the disclosure process.

INCORPORATE FEEDBACK

Pay attention to feedback received from potential Buyers and their Realtors. Use this feedback to improve your property's positioning in the market and to address concerns or issues.

ADVERTISE HOME VALUE AND BENEFITS

Use small signs, a guided tour flyer, or a recorded tour to highlight the key lifestyle values and unique features of your home. Help potential Buyers understand the lifestyle and experiences they could have here. Itemize a list of your home's updates and when they were completed. Appraisers and some Buyers appreciate how much you invested in your updates and projects. Buyers usually decide to buy based on the lifestyle they perceive they would have in the property and rationalize their decision with the list of features.

SET A COMFORTABLE STAGE

Prior to showings, turn on the lights, open curtains or blinds to maximize natural light, and create a welcoming atmosphere. Fresh cookies, bottled water or wrapped candies can be a welcome treat for people touring your home. It's best for you to leave during showings. This allows Buyers to explore freely and feel comfortable in the space. You are inviting them to imagine living in your home. If you have any home cameras monitoring the property, post a note on the door and in the listing that the home is actively being monitored.

CLEAR ACCESS TO ESSENTIAL AREAS

Ensure easy access to important areas of the home, such as the electrical panel, attic access, water shut-off valves, and crawl space. At an inspection, other areas that need easy accessibility include sump pits, water turn off, sewer cleanouts, furnace, AC, water heater, and appliances. This enables potential Buyers, their Realtors, and their inspectors to easily view these parts of your home's systems.

MAINTAIN A TIDY YARD

Keep your yard clean and well-maintained. Sweep or shovel sidewalks and driveways to remove any plant matter, snow, or ice, providing safety around the property.

By following these tips, you can create a welcoming and appealing environment for potential Buyers during live showings and increase the chances of a successful sale.

ALARM ACCESSIBILITY

If your home has an alarm system, make it easy to handle during showings. Provide clear instructions on how to operate and disable the alarm temporarily to avoid any false alarms for you and complications for potential Buyers.

SHOWING CHECKLIST

- Clean and Declutter
- Welcoming
- Our Life Suspended
- Communication

Until you get the routine down for showings, consider this checklist. Add to and subtract from this list to make it your own.

CLEAN AND DECLUTTER

01 Clutter is picked up and put away inside.

02 Clutter is picked up and put away outside.

03 Floors are swept or vacuumed.

04 Beds are made.

05 Bathrooms are clean.

06 Kitchen is clean.

07 Pet toys, dishes, poop are removed.

08 Trash is outside.

09 TV and computers are off.

WELCOMING

01 Lights are on.

02 Curtains are open.

03 Heat/cooling is set at a comfortable level.

04 Key is still in the lockbox.

05 Brochures (possibly treats) are out for Buyers.

06 The alarm is turned off or set (by the predetermined showing instructions).

OUR LIFE SUSPENDED

01 Computer is closed or off. Desk has papers put away (locked?).

02 Meds are put away.

03 Pets are kennelled or showing agents know about them in showing instructions.

04 Kids have a place to go and stay.

05 Nothing is heating on the stove or in the oven.

COMMUNICATION

01 All family members know there is a showing and to stay away for the specific time.

02 If something comes up and a showing cannot happen (ie : illness, emergency) the showing service and my Realtor are notified with a confirmation of no showings and why. Perhaps place a sign on the front door, too, in case the showing agent doesn't get the message in time.

CH. 4 WHAT IF YOUR HOME DIDN'T SELL THE FIRST TIME?

Regrouping when a Listing Expires

If your home didn't sell the first time, it is normal to be frustrated and tired. After following all the steps in the previous chapter, hopefully you have successfully sold your home. However, that is not a guarantee. In our shifting market, some homes don't sell at the first listing. If this is you, don't be discouraged. What is your plan "B"? Yesterday's Buyers didn't choose your home in its current condition and at the current price in this market. Do market trends suggest waiting for prices to go up? What would happen if you chose to rent the home for a time period? Could you achieve your bigger goals and stay in the home? If you have accepted a forbearance or have stopped paying your mortgage, tell the real estate agent you plan to hire. Both of these actions will add extra costs to close and require specific deadlines that are now being applied to your anticipated home sale.

If you still choose to sell, it's time to consider the three keys to selling a home: exposure, price and condition.

This means two of the three keys are in your control. Now is the time to regroup and evaluate what happened regarding each of these, what you learned in the previous experience, and what needs to be different to still make the move you are anticipating. Here are some steps to take.

IMPROVE EXPOSURE

Exposure is what your real estate agent provides through marketing and advertising. As the Seller, you also provide exposure by allowing access

INTERVIEW EXPERIENCED REALTORS

When relisting your home, interview Realtors who have experience selling homes that didn't sell initially. Look for a Realtor who can provide insights and strategies specific to your situation. (See the worksheet for specific questions to consider in your interview process.) Collaborating with a knowledgeable Realtor can provide you valuable guidance throughout the process.

EVALUATE YOUR IDEAL BUYERS

Consider who is the ideal Buyer for your home and how to attract that individual. Who else is an ideal Buyer for your home? What does that Buyer value? What lifestyle do they desire? How does your home fulfill these Buyer preferences? What is the value proposition your home offers the target Buyers? Discuss how to attract the target Buyers with your Realtor.

UPDATE DISCLOSURES

Address any previous inspections or issues by updating your seller property disclosures. Transparency is crucial to build trust with potential Buyers and address any concerns they may have proactively.

ADDRESS BUYER QUESTIONS

Prepare yourself to answer questions from potential Buyers about why your home didn't sell previously. Be objective and provide factual information without becoming defensive. Your Realtor will be responding to most of these questions and needs to be prepared to address them factually.

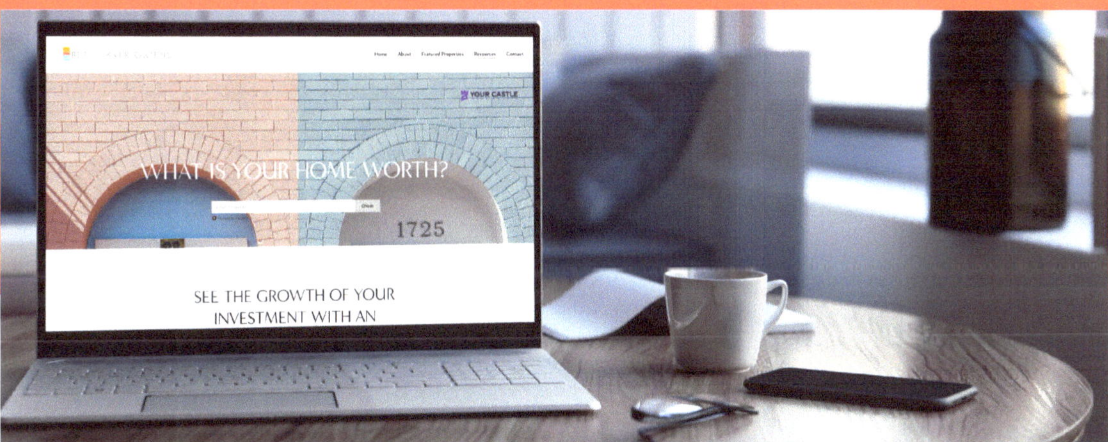

IMPROVE MARKETING EXPOSURE

Enhance the marketing efforts by improving your listing's photos, descriptions, and using other tools to attract and engage your target Buyers. How enticing is the staging and are the visuals? Would a floor plan or a 3D tour be useful? Where and how can your ideal Buyers be found? Utilize online platforms, social media, and other marketing strategies to increase exposure. Often a creative approach is good for sharing the message about the lifestyle your home offers.

PRICE

Pricing is set by applying current market trends to your specific property and is ultimately your decision.

ANALYZE SOLD HOMES

Evaluate the homes that sold and those that did not sell while your home was on the market. Deduce why specific homes sold and yours did not. Examine factors such as pricing, condition, location, and marketing strategies to identify potential areas for improvement when you relist.

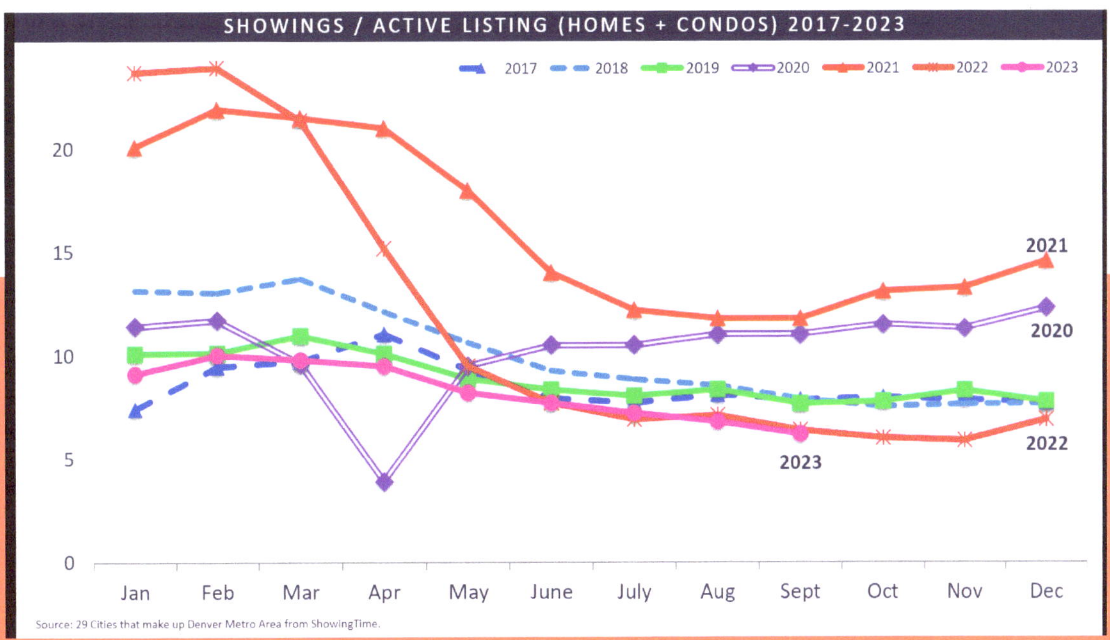

Pricing is set by applying current market trends to your specific property and is ultimately your decision.

ASSESS MARKET CONDITIONS

Understand how the real estate market has changed since your home was initially listed. Stay updated on current market trends, including inventory levels, Buyer demands, and interest rates, as these factors can influence the success of your sale. Some MLSs publish market data. Your Realtor has access to market information for the area and your specific neighborhood. As a market shifts away from being a Seller's Market, Buyers become pickier. As a market shifts away from being a Buyer's Market, Sellers don't have to offer incentives to attract Buyers. Notice how affordability has changed and how your pool of Buyers may vary.

Sometimes outside forces adjust the market, as during Covid-19 or a flood or a wildfire. Sometimes home builders affect the market. In 2023, new home builders offered strong Buyer incentives in an otherwise Seller's Market to gain an advantage over resale homes.

When interest rates are high, Sellers may offer Buyers money at closing to reduce the closing costs of the Buyers loan. Sometimes this includes an intrest rate buy down. Any seller concessions for sold properties are noted in the MLS. Ask your Realtor what is happening in your market now.

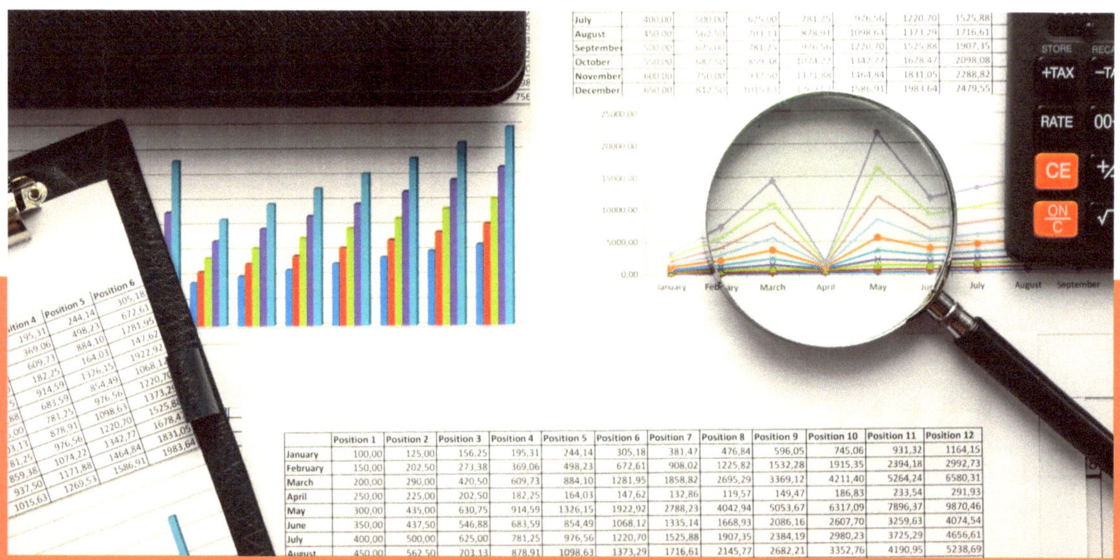

COMPARE LISTING DATA

Review the range of homes that have sold in your neighborhood and compare them to your own property. Focus on homes with a similar size, model, and age as your home. Analyze photos, condition, pricing, and exposure to gain insights into how your home can be positioned more effectively.

BUYER'S EYES TOUR

Put yourself in the shoes of a potential Buyer and go on a tour of competing listings in your area. Take note of the competing homes' strengths and weaknesses, and use this information to make improvements to your own home. A SWOT table (strengths, weaknesses, opportunities, threats) is helpful for evaluating the other properties compared to yours. Include exposure, price and condition and anything else that feels relevant. What strengths does the other home have? What weaknesses does the other home have? What are the opportunities for Buyers of this other home? What are the threats for Buyers of this other home? End the tour with a similar evaluation of your home. How does your home stack up to the competition? How can you use this information to beat the competition and sell your home?

CONDITION

Condition affects where a home fits in the market. As the Seller, you are in charge of the condition.

Maintenance matters as people consider buying a home. Disrepair deters most home buyers. They start wondering what repairs would cost. Start with a list of what maintenance is deferred in the home. Complete that honey-do list. Even when selling a home "as-is", little fixes can help a Buyer feel better about the home. Don't let your home suggest the Buyer should expect costly problems. When you hire someone to work on the home, save the receipts to provide to the Buyer later.

REVIEW PREVIOUS FEEDBACK

Based on the feedback from your previous showings, what conditions kept Buyers from bidding on your home? Was the issue cleanliness? Lack of updating? Structural concerns? A different style than is popular now? Disrepair of the home or systems? The age of major systems (heating, water heater, cooling, plumbing, electrical, roof, etc.)? Smells? It's time to be brutally honest with yourself here if you want someone to buy the home.

EVALUATE COST TO CHANGE CONDITION

Based on your analysis of the market and comparable homes, what changes would make your home a stronger competitor? Is the cost and effort of making the changes balanced out by the likely return of the property? Or is adjusting the price down a better way to put it within a competitive range? Usually a combination of addressing condition and price provides the best return on your time and financial returns.

Based on your research and analysis, you and your Realtor will reposition your home . . .

within the current market by highlighting its unique features, emphasizing its value proposition, and adjusting the price and condition to appeal to potential Buyers. When taking these steps, you can address shortcomings from your previous time on the market. Be proactive and improve the odds of selling your home successfully this second time around.

CONSIDER YOUR HOME SOLD.

NOW WHAT

- My Situation
- Price
- Condition
- Exposure

When your home didn't sell and you are still moving, here are some questions to consider.
The answers can guide you to making the adjustments you need to complete the move. Price, condition and exposure are the keys to selling any home in any market.

MY SITUATION

01 Consider what changes and different conditions I can accommodate to make my move (Timing? Renting? Way to purchase a new home? Other options?)? What is my plan B?

02 List all my concerns and experiences so far. What have I learned so far?

03 Choose an experienced Realtor to provide expertise to my team. Include these dozen questions Sellers wished they had asked the first time, gathered from three hundred people whose homes expired. Are you a full time agent and is this how you feed your family?

04 How many homes do you sell a year and how many homes have you sold in the past two years total? What is your experience selling expired listings?

05 What do you specifically do to market a previously expired listing and do you have a written marketing plan?

06 How do you acquire buyers? Do you actively prospect for buyers? If yes, can you provide me a copy of your daily work schedule and tell me specifically what you do to find Buyers?

07 What education have you taken to further yourself in Real Estate?

08 Do you have any unique advertising promotions you use to expose my home to Buyers?

09 How do you determine what's happening to the market in my neighborhood?

10 How does my home win the Buyers in this market?

MY SITUATION

11 What approach do you use when working with me to sell my home?

12 Do you provide a satisfaction guarantee?

13 How many second, in-person showings did I have?

14 How many offers did I receive and why did the Buyers terminate?

PRICE

01 How does my price/sq ft and total price compare to similar area homes that sold recently? What other factors may affect price?

02 How was my home's price set?

03 What other ways are there to value my property in today's market with the historical data available?

04 What is my required profit to make the move?

05 Could a "seller buy down" of a Buyer's loan points make a difference over a price cut? A seller "buy down" is where the seller pays money at closing for the buyer to buy points on their new mortgage to bring the interest rate down for a temporary or permanent lower rate.

CONDITION

01 What effect did condition have on the Buyers who looked at my home online and in-person, based on number of page views, showing and open house feedback, second viewing for in-person showings, inspection reports, appraisals, etc.?

02 Is there something I can do to better prepare the home for today's Buyers (Fixing deferred maintenance? Updating? Seller concessions? Specific concerns from showing feedback?)?

03 How does my home compare to the competition that got under contract while my home was active?

EXPOSURE

01 How compelling were the photos to show off my home's benefits?

02 Were showings limited and how?

03 Were there errors in the listing? How was the listing syndicated on the web?

04 Who is the right Buyer for my home? What do they want that my home has? What do they avoid that my home has?

05 To whom was the marketing directed? How did the marketing expose the right Buyer to my home? What additional ways can marketing target Buyers for my home?

"The first step to getting anywhere is deciding you're no longer willing to stay where you are."

- ANONYMOUS

As the Seller, you set up your home selling process . . .

Working with a knowledgeable Realtor, you address current market conditions, home preparations, pricing, exposure, and purchase contract steps to successfully close the sale on your home. The goal is for the Buyers to settle in and you to move on.

Start with your home. What is your home's condition? How does your home compare to the supply of other homes? What are your home's pros and cons? Is it clean and in good repair with a little glamour? You get to decide what work you want to do. Address the property's pros and cons with your Realtor. Factor in what is happening in your local market. Your neighborhood's market is not the national market, although national trends affect us all. Your local market affects pricing and timing for selling. Price and condition place your home in the marketplace for Buyers to consider. Proper exposure in the marketplace attracts the right Buyers to your home. Proper exposure is a mix of physical, digital, and interpersonal marketing. It combines positive details with property disclosures to intrigue and inform Buyers. Be sensitive to changes in your market. Make timely adjustments when conditions change.

If your home does not sell, go back dispassionately to the basics: condition, market, price, exposure. A sad reality is overpricing your home cannot be erased by excellent exposure and marketing. Money always matters to Sellers and Buyers. Make changes based on the feedback you received when you were on the market earlier. What can you address and still meet your end goals? Do your goals or the basics of condition, price, and exposure need to be adjusted? For a home to sell, Seller and Buyer (and their lender) agree about the price for the known condition of the property. The Seller and the Buyer need to feel satisfied. It is indeed satisfying as a Seller to have the cash from the closing and be able to move forward on your goals. Your home is your asset. How will you use it? When Buyers will find and choose your home by matching its condition, and price with their lifestyle dreams,

you can consider your home

SOLD.

GLOSSARY.

Appraisers: Appraisers are licensed to assess if the contract price is supported by past sales of comparable homes. For estates, the appraiser determines a value for the property on the day of the owner's death. For certain types of loans (FHA, VA or some Buyer assistance programs) an appraiser will inspect the physical condition of the property using loan standards and can require specific repairs are completed before the loan can be approved.

Buyer: A Buyer is the individual, individuals or entity interested in purchasing a home. An entity could be a trust or a Limited Liability Corporation (LLC).

Buyer's Market: A Buyer's Market occurs when there are many more properties for sale than there are Buyers. It occurs when there is more than six months of inventory of homes for sale. With more supply Buyers often have more options and can negotiate better deals.

Closing: Closing is the final step in transferring title of the property from Seller to Buyer. At closing all necessary paperwork is signed for the real estate transfer and, if used by the Buyer, loan paperwork is signed. Funds are gathered and distributed.

Closing Companies: Closing companies, known as title companies or escrow companies, facilitate the closing by gathering, creating and ensuring all the necessary documents, including the title insurance commitment, are properly prepared and executed. They also often hold the earnest money in a trust account that is specific for the transaction. Further, they manage the funds and record the documents at the county after the closing. The closing documents are delivered and recorded by the title company.

Closing Costs: The purchase contract specifies who pays HOA and other assignable fees at closing. Usual Seller closing costs include: estimated property taxes for the current year (01/01- closing date), title insurance for the purchase, title company service fee, required escrows, commissions, Seller document and recording fees, other fees stated in the purchase and listing contracts, and occasionally bills the Seller wants to pay off. Usual Buyer closing costs include fees stated in the purchase contract and a long list of loan closing costs, as specified in the Lender's Closing Disclosure (CD). Some purchase contracts include "seller concessions" that can result in shifting some of the Buyer closing costs to the Seller as an incentive or help for the Buyer.

GLOSSARY.

CPA: A CPA is a Certified Public Accountant, who specializes in financial matters, especially the tax implications related to buying and selling homes, like capital gains, 1031 exchanges, sales tax, foreign seller withholding, and others.

Deed Restrictions: Some properties have stated limitations in the warranty deed. In newer home developments, a few homes may have an income restriction. An income restriction limits how much the property may increase over time and the allowable income range of an acceptable Buyer in order to provide a few affordable homes in that development. Some deed restrictions limit the land use options for a property. Deed restrictions may expire at a certain time or continue in perpetuity.

Exclusions: Items the Seller will remove from the property when moving that may be mistaken as attached to the property, like a chandelier or a rose bush.

Feedback: Feedback is verbal or written commentary by the Buyer or Buyer's agent after looking at a property. It is usually provided after requests are made by the Seller's agent seeking what the Buyer and Buyer's agent thought about the property's condition and price and what questions they may have about the property.

For Sale By Owners (FSBO): FSBOs are properties that are being marketed directly by the Sellers to the Buyers.

Home Equity Line of Credit (HELOC): A home equity line of credit is a second mortgage given to the Seller. Sometimes it is used and sometimes not used. Regardless of the balance on the loan, a HELOC needs to be paid off and closed by the lender of the second mortgage when the property is transferred to the Buyer. Sometimes it or its payoff is not recorded at the county. It is the Seller's responsibility to tell their Realtor about past and present HELOCs when evaluating what the Seller's estimated proceeds will be at closing.

Homeowners Association (HOA): An organization that manages common areas and services and enforces rules and regulations for properties in a specific development. There may be multiple HOAs for a single property. HOAs also charge fees at closing for a status letter on the homeowner's account and for transferring the account to the Buyer. Who pays these fees should be specified in the purchase contract. An HOA may charge a special assessment for unexpected expenses or major community improvements. Special assessments or discussions about possibly having one need to be disclosed by the Seller to the Buyer.

GLOSSARY.

Home Warranty: This service contract covers repairs or replacement of specific home systems and appliances if something fails or breaks later. There is a fee for service and the home warranty company specifies the limits of coverage and which contractors may make the evaluation of the problem and make the repair.

Inclusion: Item that is not part of the structure that the Seller transfers to the Buyer with a Bill of Sale at closing.

Inspection: An examination of a property to determine qualities of a property at the time of the visual inspection. Inspections can be of a specific system, like a sewer scope or a structural evaluation or a radon test. General home inspections address the overall function of the structure and major systems, like plumbing, electric, HVAC, etc. An Inspection Report can vary from a couple of notes to a comprehensive document with photos, concerns, current standards and suggestions for later attention. Inspectors are not licensed, but many belong to the two professional organizations: InterNACHI and ASHI.

Investors: Individuals or entities who purchase properties with the goal of generating income (making a profit through rental income and property appreciation) or renovation and resale (called fix and flip). Some entities are LLCs for individuals, others are parts of larger corporate interests.

Lead-Based Paint Disclosure (LBP): This disclosure is required for all homes built during or before 1978. In it the Seller discloses if they have tested for or have knowledge of lead based paint applied to the property. The Buyer discloses if they want to test for lead based paint or waive their right to test for lead in the paint. Eating paint chips or breathing in dust from lead based paint can cause serious health problems, especially for infants and children. For more information about lead poisoning read https://www.epa.gov/lead/protect-your-family-sources-lead.

Leased or Encumbered Inclusions: Some inclusions require disclosure because the Buyer needs to agree to the inclusion's additional expense and agreements with other people. One common inclusion is solar panels. If they are not owned outright, the Seller is either leasing them or buying them with a loan and has written, binding agreements with the solar company and the utility company regarding their solar panels. The Buyer needs to qualify for and agree to the extra expense. Some of the expenses include increased insurance costs and agreements with the solar company and the utility company. A propane tank and a security system with monitoring are other examples of inclusions that are often leased by the Seller and have ongoing agreements the Buyer will be bound to after closing.

GLOSSARY.

Lender: The individual or institution that funds part of the Buyer's home purchase. Mortgage loans and lenders all have specific requirements before they will give a Buyer the funding. Beyond income, debt, appraisal and title requirements, there are often property condition requirements.

Market Conditions: The current state of the real estate market as measured by number of homes listed, number of homes pending, number of homes sold, days in MLS, days to purchase contract, seller concessions, price changes, interest rates, seasonality, the general economy, and specific happenings in the area.

Mineral Rights: Some properties have mineral rights still attached to the land. The title insurance commitment addresses mineral rights tied to a property. Often the surface rights of an owner to live, build buildings, grow crops, put in a well or septic system are severed from the rights to explore, remove, and sell natural resources under the soil surface. Sometimes mineral rights change the value of a property. Some properties have recorded gas and oil rights under the surface. If so, this information is supposed to be disclosed by the Seller to the Buyer. Consult your Realtor about this and engage the proper professional assistance as needed. A land man is used to help value mineral rights and to transfer them. Rules for this vary by state.

Months of Inventory (MOI): Measure of how fast homes are selling in the market. MOI = (# homes active on the market)/(# homes sold in a month). A Seller's market is less than six MOI. A Buyer's market is more than six MOI.

Owner & Encumbrance (O&E): Report from a title company with owners' names, owners' mailing address and all recorded liens.

Pre-Inspection: A general home inspection requested by the Seller to determine what can be addressed prior to marketing a home for sale. The report is supposed to be disclosed to Buyers. Coupled with receipts and other documentation of work completed, a Buyer can feel assured the home is well maintained.

Purchase Contract: A legally binding contract between Seller and Buyer that states the property, price, terms, inclusions, exclusions, due diligence dates, and deadlines for the agreement. Additional provisions may also address other concerns of the Seller and Buyer, like Seller Concessions or Seller Rent Back.

GLOSSARY.

Radon: A colorless, odorless, dense, naturally occurring gas created when radioactive uranium decays. An alpha emitter. Common in many Colorado homes. Has been correlated to lung cancer in many studies. Colorado requires all radon test results and any radon mitigation systems installed on a property must be disclosed by Sellers.

Rate Buy Down: When interest rates are high, the rate can be bought down at closing. There are temporary buy downs that decrease the mortgage payment for the first one or two years the Buyer owns the home. A permanent buy down costs more and decreases the rate for the life of the loan. A Buyer's lender can calculate the cost of a buy down when the Buyer locks their interest rate for a loan.

Realtor: A licensed real estate agent who is a member of the National Association of Realtors and adheres to a code of ethics.

Relocation Services: Some employers offer benefits to employees who have work-related moves. Each relocation package is different and needs to be read and the parameters followed carefully. Usually there is additional documentation provided to the relocation service provider before, during, and after the closing to keep communication clear with this entity. Further, there may be rules for: marketing, addressing property conditions, market conditions, pricing, timing, and care of the property if the Seller leaves before closing.

Seller Concessions: Funds credited from the Seller to the Buyer at closing. These closing costs show up on the Seller's Settlement Statement as a debit. Seller concessions may be applied to paying for some of the loan closing costs or a rate buy down for the Buyer.

Seller Disclosures: In most real estate transactions, the Seller provides several disclosures for the Buyer. Ask your Realtor which are standard in your area. Standard disclosures include important facts the Seller knows about the property, like square footage, if lead based paint was used on the property, well permits, etc. Especially important to disclose are "material defects" in a property that could affect its value, usability or safety.

Seller's Market: A Seller's Market occurs when there are more Buyers than there are properties for sale. It occurs when there is less than six months of inventory of homes for sale. With less supply Sellers often have more options and can negotiate better deals.

GLOSSARY.

Seller Property Disclosure (SPD): Disclosure form commonly used for the Seller to disclose facts and some possible adverse material defects in the property. Sometimes additional disclosures are needed to disclose more facts about a specific condition on the property. These could be engineering or site reports, receipts for work performed, insurance claims, etc.

Stager: An interior designer who helps the Seller prepare the home for sale. A traditional stager offers a variety of services from suggestions to renting furniture to setting up and removing the furniture and decor. A virtual stager changes a vacant home's photos.

Title Insurance Commitment: At closing there are two title insurance policies: one the Seller provides to the Buyer and one that the Buyer provides to their lender. Title insurance is used by Buyers and lenders for protection against back taxes, undisclosed liens, legal judgements, forgeries, fraud, other possible legal or financial problems that could result from purchasing a property. It is required in Colorado.

Vacant Home: A property that is currently unoccupied. Meaning, without any residents nor tenants.

Water Source & Rights: Disclosure of the water source for a property is important. Some properties have no water. Others have city water. Wells require extra steps in a real estate transaction. Raw land and agricultural land may have additional water rights that are also sold with the property. If so, this information needs to be disclosed by the Seller to the Buyer. Selling water rights requires extra steps and uses a water lawyer. Consult your Realtor about this and engage the proper professional.

ACKNOWLEDGMENTS.

This is a distillation of almost 30 years of working with sellers in a variety of markets, and succussfully moving them forward to their next home.

Many thanks to my husband, Kent, a fellow Realtor who taught me the ropes back in 1997 when we started working together as a team. For this edition, Kent, Joe Massey, Megan Beach have provided valuable feedback. Heartfelt thanks to my daughter, Kelsey Owens for her work taking the manuscript and putting it into this esthetically pleasing format. Finally, thanks to you dear reader for taking time to make your sale smoother by thinking ahead. This way you will be as prepared as possible to have a smooth transaction. The devil's in the details and every transaction is a little different from the others. As Churchill said," Plans are of little importance, but planning is essential."

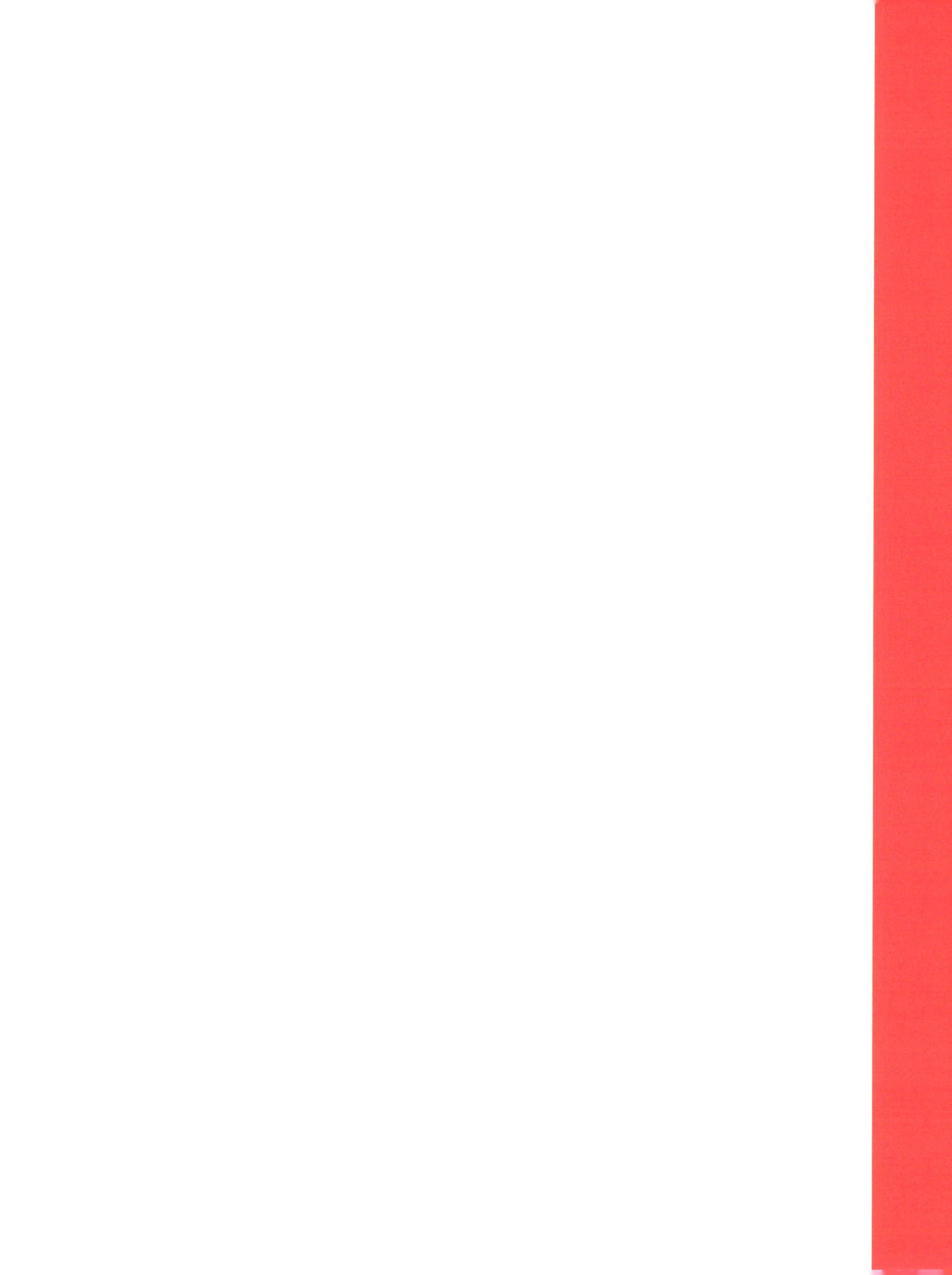

ABOUT
The author.

Beth Baker Owens moved to Denver in 1977 to attend the University of Denver on a Boettcher Scholarship. After receiving an MBA, she joined her husband as a Realtor in 1997. She has spent the last 30 years serving the great Denver Metro Area as one of the leading faces in real estate. She uses her background in professional coaching to provide a customized approach for her clients. This allows for them to clarify their goals and acheive them in today's market. She teaches multiple classes annually to real estate agents, buyers, and sellers. She works with the Boettcher Foundation Alumni Board and a variety of community projects. Fond of being in the mountains, she also enjoys gardening, reading, cooking with her husband, and being with family.

www.ingramcontent.com/pod-product-compliance
Ingram Content Group UK Ltd.
Pitfield, Milton Keynes, MK11 3LW, UK
UKHW060117300726
14090UKWH00002B/244

* 9 7 9 8 8 9 3 7 9 1 7 3 0 *